Before You Were Here

WRITTEN BY
Scott Westerfeld

ILLUSTRATED BY
Jessica Lanan

Roaring Brook Press
New York

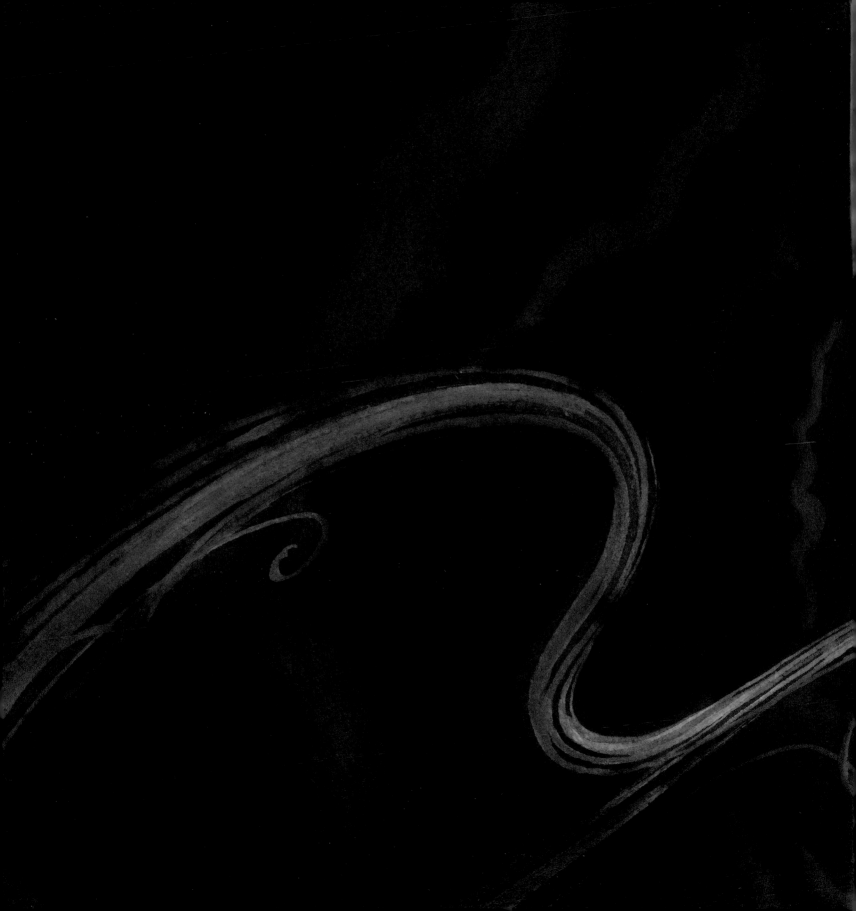

Before you were here,
you were waiting . . .

everywhere.

You were once the sunshine
when it struck the trees,
sweetening their fruit,
kindling the energy that flows through you.

Your muscles lift
and flex with light.

You were also the rain,
gathering in torrents,
rivers, oceans,
soft and cool on the skin.

Our world is mostly sea, and you are mostly water, powerful enough to wear away mountains.

Some of you was waiting deep in the earth,
ready to be drawn up by the roots of plants.

Your blood is red with iron.
Calcium hardens your bones, fingernails,
and teeth. Sodium and potassium carry
sparks of electricity inside you.

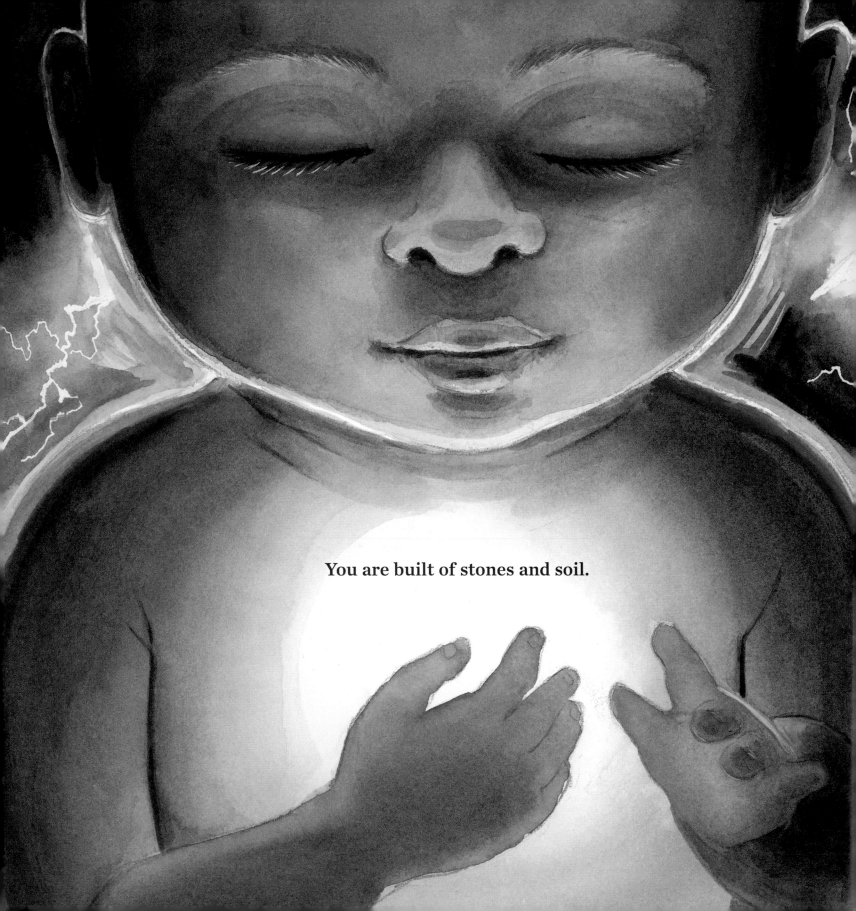

You are built of stones and soil.

A piece of you waited
in every living thing,
instructions woven
into every cell.

You share this code with dogs
and cats, plants and earthworms,
chimpanzees swinging from branches,
and other humans too.

The ticktock of the living world
helped fashion you.

And now that you're here, growing bigger, stronger, more beautiful, you are still the sunshine. You are still the rain, the earth, the pulse of life.

And the world still waits for you . . .

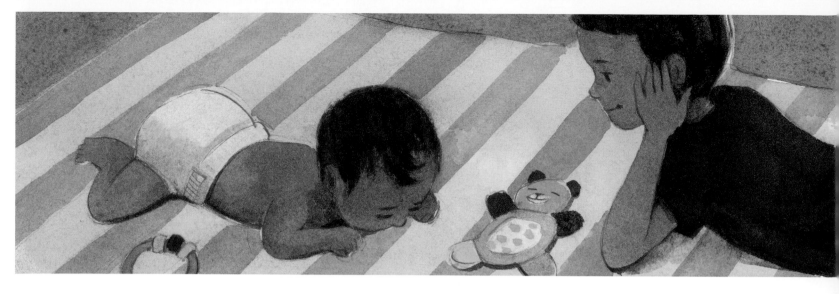

everywhere.

Our bodies are made of ordinary things, like water and minerals, and are brought to life by the energy in sunlight. *Before You Were Here* explains where these components come from and how they connect us to the physical world. Read on to learn the science behind this book.

You were once the sunshine . . .

Almost all life on Earth is powered by the sun. Plants use a process called photosynthesis to convert the energy from sunlight into chemical forms, like sugars and starches. When we eat plants and animals, this energy passes into us, making all of our bodily functions possible. Every footstep, every heartbeat, every growth spurt can be traced back to the sun.

You were also the rain . . .

Water covers much of the world. Your body is made mostly of water, and life first evolved in the sea. The water within us cushions and protects our organs and joints, regulates our temperature, and helps us absorb nutrients. We can't last more than a few days without it, and drinking enough water is a key part of staying healthy.

Some of you was waiting deep in the earth . . .

Minerals are drawn up into the living world by plant roots deep in the soil. Minerals compose only about 4 percent of your body, but there are at least fifteen different types that perform specific functions inside you. Iron helps transport oxygen in your blood. Sodium and potassium are electrolytes, which carry the electrical signals of your brain, nerves, and muscles.

A piece of you waited in every living thing . . .

Each cell in a living organism contains DNA, a set of chemical instructions needed to create and maintain that organism. Humans share sequences of this code with every form of life, from earthworms (about 70 percent the same DNA as humans) to chimpanzees (about 98 percent the same). When a child is conceived, the parents' DNA combines into a new set of instructions to create that unique human being.

Your connection to the universe didn't stop when you were born. Every minute of every day, water, minerals, and energy pass between your body and the world around you. You are a part of that world no matter where you go.

To Dany — S. W.

For Lexi and Mav —J. L.

Published by Roaring Brook Press
Roaring Brook Press is a division of Holtzbrinck Publishing Holdings Limited Partnership
120 Broadway, New York, NY 10271 • mackids.com

Our books may be purchased in bulk for promotional, educational, or business use.
Please contact your local bookseller or the Macmillan Corporate and Premium Sales Department
at (800) 221-7945 ext. 5442 or by email at MacmillanSpecialMarkets@macmillan.com.

Library of Congress Control Number 2023043416

First edition, 2024
The illustrations in this book were created using ink, watercolor, and gouache.
The type was set in Chronicle. The book was edited by Emily Feinberg, with design by Mike Burroughs
and art direction by Sharismar Rodriguez. The assistant editor was Emilia Sowersby. The production editor
was Jennifer Healey, and the production was supervised by Celeste Cass.
Printed in China by Toppan Leefung Printing Ltd., Dongguan City, Guangdong Province.

ISBN 978-1-250-79932-6

1 3 5 7 9 10 8 6 4 2